Seven Steps To Empower Your Faith

By

Josephine Brooks - Clark

Seven Steps To Empower Your Faith

By

Josephine Brooks - Clark

Copyright @ 2015, All Rights Reserved
Printed in The United States of America

Published By:

ABM Publications
A division of Andrew Bills Ministries Inc.
PO Box 6811, Orange, CA 92863

www.abmpublications.com

ISBN: 978-1-931820-59-2

All scripture quotations, unless otherwise indicated are taken from the King James Version of the Bible, Public Domain. Those marked AMP are from the Amplified Bible, copyright @ 1987, The Updated Edition, by the Zondervan Corporation and the Lockman Foundation, and is used by permission. All rights reserved.

DEDICATION

To my daughters and grandchildren

Prophetess Felecia Harris
Prophetess Valorie Baker
Kevin J. Clark
Glenn Baker Jr
Eric Harris
Krea Baker
Melanie Rowe
R'Hasia Baker
Anton Rowe and
Corryn Baker

They will be a part of that great host of men & women that will proclaim the gospel.

SEVEN STEPS TO EMPOWER YOUR FAITH

TABLE OF CONTENTS

	About The Author	7
1	Let Not Your Heart Be Troubled	9
2	You Must Encourage Yourself	13
3	I Will Show You A Mystery	17
4	When Ye Drink Any Deadly Thing	19
5	Faith As The Grain Of A Mustard Seed	21
6	Faith Without Works Is Dead	23
7	Pray And Believe	29
	The Steps Of A Warrior	31
	Description Of Faith	33
	Faith Is Of Degrees	35
	Ground Of Belief	37
	Responsibility Of Faith	39
	Examples Of Faith	41
	7 Steps To Empower Your Faith – pt 2	43

SEVEN STEPS TO EMPOWER YOUR FAITH

ABOUT THE AUTHOR

Evangelist Josephine Clark was born in Birmingham, Alabama into a family of 11 children, 7 girls and 4 boys in which I am a twin. I am formerly educated in Birmingham Alabama, after graduation, I moved to Chicago, Illinois. I attended Olive Harvey Jr College & Bryant Stratton Business College. Later on attended Colorado Technical University, graduated with a Master in Business Administration.

I began to answer my call as an Evangelist in 1965, also not understanding the call, of a vision I had one Sunday Morning while sitting in church, it was as if the roof of the church building had literally opened up and I saw the bible handed down to me, and this scripture was given for me to read, St Mark 16:15-18, "AND HE SAID UNTO THEM, GO YE INTO ALL THE World, AND PREACH THE GOSPEL TO EVERY CREATURE. HE THAT BELIEVETH AND IS BAPTIZED SHALL BE SAVED: BUT HE THAT BELIEVETH NOT SHALL BE DAMNED. AND THESE SIGNS SHALL FOLLOWE THEM THAT BELIEVE: IN MY NAME SHALL THEY CAST OUT DEVILS: THEY SHALL SPEAK WITH NEW TONGUES: THEY SHALL TAKE UP SERPENTS; AND IF THEY DRINK ANY

DEADLY THING, It SHALL NOT HURT THEM, THEY SHALL LAY HANDS ON THE SICK, AND THEY SHALL RECOVER.

As I continued to grow in the knowledge of the word, I then realized that I was being called into the ministry. I started going to Nursing Homes and being trained on the Evangelist field at the age of 20 years old, under the leadership of the Late Bishop Goldsberry, Faith Temple Church of God in Christ.

By the time I was 30, I moved my membership to Old Land Mark Church of God Holiness In Christ, under the leadership of Apostle Mitchell. That is where I learned to submit to authority, obey them that have the rule over you. I learned to preach and exhort on God's word.

In 1979 I was ordained an Elder and later on about 1984, my husband and I left and became working together in ministry. In 1985 my husband and I started our own ministry, Miracle Deliverance Outreach Ministry. In 1995 Pastor Rudy became Ill and I was ordained the Pastor. The Holy Spirit has been in operation since, moving through signs and wonders.

STEP ONE:

LET NOT YOUR HEARTS BE TROUBLED (ST JOHN 14:1 NIV)

St John 14:1" Do not let your heart be troubled, trust in God, and trust also in me. In my father's house are many rooms: if it were not so, I would have told you. I am going there, to prepare a place for you, and if I go and prepare a place for you I will come back and take you to be with me that you also may be where I am. You know the way to the place where I am going." Since Jesus is saying, "do not let your heart to be trouble, you may have just received some alarming news, and now your heart is troubled. Jesus is also saying there is an antidote for your problem:

EXAMPLE: Faith testimony:

TESTIMONY ONE:

Pastor and I were in a conference 2000. We had been sowing, sowing, and sowing; we also sowed a portion of our rent for the month, trusting in God to work a miracle. The note on our cars were due, two months behind on rent, parking space due, and storage fee were due.

This was a time that we needed God to prove himself to us, that if we sacrifice to him, a sacrificial offering, he will do just what his word say, Luke 6:38, : Give, and it will be given to you. A good measure, pressed down, and shaken together and running over, will be poured into your lap. For with the measure you use, it will be measure to you". We needed God to prove himself to us. All of the bills too were due, the cars, the dealer waived the two months, and rent that was due, we only had to come up with one month. So by the middle of the month, we started receiving money, that total up to $3600.00 dollars. PRAISE GOD, GOD spoke to our hearts and blessed us when we were in trouble.

TESTIMONY TWO:

Arthur W. Brooks Sr. had been diagnosis with crippling arthritis, being used by God, going in and out of four prisons in Alabama. "Papa" is what we called him and we knew he had to be delivered.

Papa Brooks talked to God about his condition. One morning while sitting in his rocking chair, God spoke to him to drink OLIVE OIL. Papa Brooks began taking just 1 teaspoon of oil, the second time around God spoke; "WHY LIMIT ME!"

God wanted Papa Brooks to drink the whole bottle of olive oil. From that day forward after drinking the whole bottle, Papa Brooks was miraculously healed of crippling arthritis. PRAISE GOD another step of faith.

JOSEPHINE BROOKS - CLARK

STEP TWO:

YOU MUST ENCOURAGE YOURSELF
(I SAMUEL 30:6)

"AND DAVID WAS GREATLY DISTRESSED; FOR THE PEOPLE SPAKE OF STONING HIM, BECAUSE THE SOUL OF ALL THE PEOPLE WAS GRIEVED, EVERY MAN FOR HIS SONS AND FOR HIS DAUGHTERS; BUT DAVID ENCOURAGED HIMSELF IN THE LORD HIS GOD".

Knowing what all David went thru, houses being burned down, his wives and sons taken captive, after all this, can we say we still love and trust the Lord, I love you Lord with all my heart. What if your children were taken from you, husband leave, and house go into foreclosure, car dealer take your car, and you lose your job. Is the praises of the Father still in your mouth.

TESTIMONY:

By this time our daughters were in the 4th and 6th grades. The girls were at home with their dad watching television. I had just come in from night school taking classes in accounting.

As I spoke to the girls and Rudy, four young men used a crow bar to break into our apartment. As they entered the apartment, one stated, "THIS IS A STICK UP". I was in the bedroom, picked up the phone and screamed, "Did you say this was a stick up?" The security officer from downstairs was on the other end of the phone, talking to me to get my car repaired when he heard them say, "This is a stick up."

One tied Rudy up, two were in the room with my daughters and the other one entered the room where I was and ask for money and jewelry. PRAISE GOD, I only had $50.00 and my diamond ring. I gave it to the young man. I began to tell the young man, "You do not look like a murderer." But he told me, "Shut your mouth because you don't know what you're talking about."

I kept talking and then I started to witness to the young man. He did not know what to say so he left me alone. By that time the policemen were in the building, the young men escaped down the back stairs, one jumped over the banister.

While the policemen chased the men, they were able to catch three, but the driver of the car got away. On the day of the trial, one of my daughters did not testify, but when she saw one of the men with his green snake skin shoes on, she remembered that he was the one that had held the gun to her head.

While in court, they were found guilty and were sentenced to 25 years without the possibility of parole.

STEP THREE:

I WILL SHOW YOU A MYSTERY (I CORINTHIANS 15:51)

BEHOLD, I WILL SHOW YOU A MYSTERY; WE SHALL NOT ALL SLEEP, BUT SHALL ALL BE CHANGED….

Mystery - I have learned the secret, manifested the operation of those hidden forces. The mystery, we will not all sleep, is in references to death, found in the Lord's remarks concerning Jarius' daughter. The sleep refers to the death of the body, but only of such as are Christ; yet never of Christ Himself, though he is the first-fruit of them that have fallen asleep.

I CORINTHIANS 15:20 BUT NOW IS CHRIST RISEN FROM THE DEAD, AND BECOME THE FIRST-FRUITS OF THEM THAT SLEPT. Of Lazarus, while Christ was yet upon the earth, John 11:11, "THESE THINGS SAID HE; AND AFTER THAT HE SAITH UNTO THEM, OUR FRIEND LAZARUS SLEEPETH; BUT I GO, THAT I MAY AWAKE HIM OUT OF SLEEP".

Daniel 12:2 informs us that the physical body is described of them that are asleep in the dust of the earth. "Dust" denotes to ruin, or to destroy. A language inappropriate (unsuitable) to the spiritual part of man; moreover, when the body who returns whence it came in Genesis 3:19b, for out of it wast thou taken; for dust thou art; and unto dust shall thou return. The spirit returns to God who gave it. Ecclesiastes 12:7. Then shall the dust return to the earth as it was; and the spirit shall return unto God who gave it" man's body will return to the dust, the spirit return unto God, man's spirit to God for Judgment.

STEP FOUR:

WHEN YE DRINK ANY DEADLY THING (ST. MARK 16:18b)

"THEY SHALL TAKE UP SERPENTS, AND IF THEY DRINK ANY DEADLY THING, IT SHALL NOT HURT THEM; THEY SHALL LAY HANDS ON THE SICK, AND THEY SHALL RECOVER".

The New Testament records no instance of anyone drinking poison without harm. LUKE 10; 19a stated that Jesus will give you power to tread over serpents and scorpions; when we metaphorically are treading underfoot the enemy; the Son of God as used in Hebrews 10:29b, who hath trodden underfoot the Son of God; he was insulted, outraged, describing the sin of unbelief.

They turned away from God to indulge in willful sin. Serpent meaning that which is evil, he will caution you to avoid danger; its treachery; its venom, and its murderous proclivities meaning you are capable of murdering with the mind. Psalms 58:4a" their poison is like the poison of a serpent" because of inborn sinfulness, men lie, poison others with words and are deaf to all appeals (just as a snake who will not obey a snake charmer).

Proverbs 23:32, "at the last it biteth like a serpent, and stingeth like and adder". The scorpion is a small animal, just like a lobster, but with a long tail, at the end of which has a venomous sting, the pain in Revelation 9:3, 5, & 10, tells you about the position of the sting and its effect. The Lord assured the disciples in St Luke 10:19 of the authority given unto them by Him to tread upon serpents and scorpions, conveys the thought of Victory over spiritual forces that will oppose you, the power of darkness which is power of the enemy.

STEP FIVE

FAITH AS THE GRAIN OF A MUSTARD SEED (MATTHEW 17; 20b)

We know that the mustard seed is among the smallest seeds. As long as the seed is tiny, it produces small faith, more word, more faith, more experience, and more growth. So as the seed began to produce strength and growth your faith began to rise to a level of maturity. You have then an unusual reliance on God. How do we produce a little bit of faith? If ye have faith and doubt not, ye shall be able to speak that which is impossible into your life. You must ask in prayer, believe, then ye shall receive.

When Pastor Clark and I got married, it had been stated by doctors, I will never have children. I spent money after money, running from one specialist to another, only to hear the same story.

Get this from the doctor, **"Mother you might as well live with the fact, that you will never have children".**

Bishop Goldberry of Faith Temple Church of God in Christ laid hands on Rudy and I, spoke these words over our life, "GO DAUGHTER BELIEVING GOD FOR YOUR MIRACLE".

STEP SIX

FAITH WITHOUT WORKS IS DEAD

JAMES 2:26; "FOR AS THE BODY WITHOUT SPIRIT IS DEAD, SO FAITH WITHOUT WORKS IS DEAD ALSO". HEBREWS 11:1 "NOW FAITH IS THE SUBSTANCE OF THINGS HOPE FOR AND THE EVIDENCE OF THINGS NOT SEEN"

Sometimes things must happen in our lives in order for works to manifest. Faith is when you don't actually see what is taken place in your life, knowing that God has said: if you have the faith of the size of a mustard seed, you can speak it that mountain in your life; meaning lifting itself above the plain; so speak to your situation and lift yourself up and above what you are going through. You must go through the fire, after you have gone through, you will come out as pure gold. In order to shine as gold you must be tired in the earth furnace, purified seven times. God's words are as pure and valuable as silver is being fully refined.

JAMES 2:17-18 "EVEN SO FAITH, IF IT HAS NOT WORKS, IS DEAD BEING ALONE. YEA, A MAN MAY

SAY, THOU HAST FAITH, AND I HAVE WORKS; SHEW ME THOU FAITH WITHOUT THY WORKS, AND I WILL SHEW THEE MY FAITH BY MY WORKS".

Faith and works, the inquiry.

Can a non-working, dead spurious faith save a person? In the book of James, the second chapter he not saying that we are saved by works, but that faith that does not produce good works is a dead faith. The Apostle Pail and James describe faith as a living, productive trust in Christ. When you have genuine faith, it cannot be dead or barren to works. Talking about spurious faith read James 2:15-16. If faith has no works is dead being alone, and then show me your faith which will produce you some works.

VALORIE'S TESTIMONY:

In 1985 I found out that I had peptic ulcer. I was 15 years old and dying. I was pale yellow and hearing sounds that sounded like crickets in my ears. I got ill at school and the nurse called my parents to say I was ill. I was rushed to the emergency room, the nurse tried pricking my finger for blood there was no blood that came out except a little from my thumb. The doctor said I was a walking corpse. They did not understand how I was alive, no blood in my veins. I had been bleeding internally for about a week.

The doctors wanted to give me a blood transfusion, because AIDS was a big epidemic then, and my mother refused to let them give me a transfusion. They made her sign papers that if I died, it would be their fault. My mother began to pray as she lied in the hospital bed with me for a week. I recovered during the night; it was as if an angel came into the room and place blood in my veins. I still did not believe that God was going to heal me; I had to come to God on my knees.

After I got married, and had my four children the same thing began to happen again. This time I knew that I was dying, I felt my spirit leave my body. A week before this happen, a prophet told me that God said, "all of my troubles were about to be over". I just wanted that prophet to go away and leave me along. She began to do spiritual warfare around me and it felt as if I was in the middle of a whirlwind. A week later my husband said he saw a man in the hallway in my bedroom looking at me. He could not see his face, but he knew he was looking at me.

When I woke up the next morning and I knew my life was over if I did not start praying. I called my mother and sister to come and pray for me, because I felt I couldn't do it on my own. As I lied there on the floor they began to pray and the glory of God came into my body and I had unknown energy. I still went to the hospital and when I got there they found 6 more ulcers building up in my body. The hospital kept me for a week and gave me this time a blood transfusion. I had faith that it was God's will. I am now Ulcer free. I am also a minister in the gospel and know that God is real.

The Late Bliss Pope

TESTIMONY TWO:

This man, Bliss was considered dead. He had been in a coma for three (3) long months, doctor's stated he will not recover, damage is serious beyond compare. If by chance he did survive, he will become a vegetable. He will not be able to function as a full man. 'BUT MY GOD THAT SITS

HIGH AND LOOK LOW" looked upon this man and said, THY SHALL LIVE AND NOT DIE. Mother Brooks had all of the children to fast and pray, we had to go to school with no food, we had to pray because we wanted to see our brother-in-law live. The reason we had to fast, Bliss was hit by an 18 wheeler truck while station in Germany, United States Army. Bliss was pinned in between the front end of his car, had to be cut out before the car would blow up. It is just amazing how God works. After the fast, Bliss recovered, came out of the coma, had children, found a job and began his journey serving the Lord. What a miracle, no brain damage, nothing wrong with his organs to produce and able to be a good husband to his wife.

PRAISE GOD FOR SUCH A GREAT OUTCOME. WITH GOD NOTHING IS IMPOSSILE IF YE ONLY BELIEVE.

STEP SEVEN

PRAY AND BELIEVE

MARK 11; 24" THEREFORE, I SAY UNTO YOU, WHAT THINGS SOEVER YE DESIRE, WHEN YE PRAY, BELIEVE THAT YE RECEIVE THEM, AND YE SHALL HAVE THEM".

When we pray and believe, we actually are removing the difficulties that will arise in our life. When ye pray you must believe your prayers are being heard, ye must have a relationship with Him. Every act of faith must rest on the promises of God.

If we know that it is God's will to remove difficulties then we can pray with confidence that it will be done. We can have that assurance of answered prayer before the answer comes. Matthews 7:7, "ask, and it shall be given you; seek, and ye shall find, knock, and it shall be opened unto you:

TESTIMONY

After prayer, Pastor Rudy and I believe God for a

child. When doctors kept saying there was no way to have a baby, but God answer prayer. My God will supply all of your needs if ye only believe. After my second daughter was born, the enemy started fighting us again for the lives of my daughter.

The battle really got intense, when she was six months old, she was attacked with spinal meningitis, once 3rd degree burn on her left leg and then suffered with ulcers, and she felled and hit her head and was blind for a short period of time.

When Valorie hit her head, she was young, but she spoke to me and said, mom, stop crying and start praying for my eyes so I may see. No matter what, the war was on with the enemy. Praise God, both daughters are at this presence married and have wonderful husbands.

II CORINTHIANS 10: 4 "FOR THE WEAPONS OF OUR WARFARE ARE NOT CARNAL, BUT MIGHTY THROUGH GOD, TO THE PULLING DOWN STRONG HOLDS.

PRAISE GOD FOR HIS WONDERFUL RESOURCES.

THE STEPS OF A WARRIOR

This is learned

Combat basic martial art to defend

Disguise charge at all times

Stealth learn how to walk silently

This is training

Be physically fit

Practice work on strategies

Train like a ninja: work out daily

Never give up: You must last till the end

JOSEPHINE BROOKS - CLARK

DESCRIPTION OF FAITH

Faith is accompanied by love	show it	Ephesians 3:16
Faith is commendable	mention it	Hebrews 11:1
Faith is complete	having it all	Matthew 13:44
Faith is fruitful	bearing fruit	1 Thessalonians 1:3
Faith is a gift	you receive it	Romans 12:3
Faith is like a breastplate	you wear it	1 Thessalonians 5:8

JOSEPHINE BROOKS - CLARK

FAITH IS OF DEGREES
ETERNAL BENEFITS OF FAITH
JOHN 20:29

A benefit of faith is adoption to become the legal guardian into the body of Christ Galatians 3:26

A benefit of faith is assurance Hebrews 10:22

A benefit of faith is confidence and freedom from doubt I Peter 2:6

A benefit of faith is eternal life John 3:16

A benefit of faith is inheriting the promise Hebrews 6:12

A benefit of faith is rewarding II Timothy 4:7

That which is an advantage

Advantage & benefit both mean that which is of value

Access to God is a benefit of faith. Eph 3:12

Yeshua indwelling is a benefit of faith.

Eph 3:16-17

Divine blessing is a benefit of faith. Ps 40:4

Divine empowering (to give power or authority to) is a benefit of faith. Matt 17:20

God's Love is a benefit of faith. Ps 32:10

Grace is a benefit of faith. Romans 5:1

Joy is a benefit of faith. Acts 16:34

Worshiping and praising Yahweh is evidence of faith. Psalm 106:11, Exodus 4:29

GROUNDS OF BELIEF – EVIDENCES OF TRUE FAITH

Demonstrating the Fruit of the Spirit is evidence of faith. Gal 5:22

Encouraging others in the faith is evidence of faith. Titus 1:1

Fearing Yahweh God is evidence of faith. Exodus 14:31

Growing spiritually is evidence of faith. II Thes 1:3

Living in accordance to faith is evidence of faith. I Thes 1:3; James 2:14-15

Loving others is evidence of faith. Eph 1:15

Proclaiming Yahweh's message to others is evidence of faith. Acts 20:21

Worshiping and praising Yahweh is evidence of faith. Ps 106:11; Ps 28:7; Exodus 4:29

JOSEPHINE BROOKS - CLARK

RESPONSIBILITY OF FAITH BEING ACCOUNTABLE

One must continue in faith   II Corinthians 13; 5

One must excel in faith II Corinthians 8:7 just as ye excel in everything in faith, in speech, in knowledge, in complete earnestness and in you love.

One must hold fast the faith II Timothy 1:19

One must remain strong in the faith I Corinthians 16:13. Be on your guard, stand firm in the faith, be strong and of good courage.

JOSEPHINE BROOKS - CLARK

EXAMPLES OF FAITH

Abel: by faith Abel offered unto God a better sacrifice than Cain

Enoch: by faith Enoch was taken from this life so that he did not experience death

Noah: by faith Noah when warned about things not yet seen in fear built an ark

Abraham: by faith Abraham even though he was past age and Sarah herself was barren was able to become a father.

Job: through the slay me, yet will I trust in him

Peter: Simon Peter answered you are the Messiah the Son of the Living God

Eunice: I have been reminded of your sincere faith, which first lived in your grandmother Lois, and in your mother Eunice and I am persuaded that same faith now lives in you also.

JOSEPHINE BROOKS - CLARK

SEVEN STEPS TO EMPOWER YOUR FAITH

PART 2

Let's take each one of the seven steps and began to peel them apart, one by one as if they were an orange. What are you saying? When you peel an orange, just how do you peel? You cut a hole in the top so that the sides of the orange can be peeled without making a mess and spilling the juice. Seven steps of faith will be peeled into sections one by one and see what God (Yahweh) is saying.

1. **Let not your heart be troubled;** why Jesus (Yashua) would speak those words to such a dying world. Knowing that the heart is the chief organ of the physical life (for life of the flesh is in the blood). Leviticus 17:11a which occupies the most important place in the system of the human body. Therefore, the heart stands for both the rational and emotional elements. The heart also stands for man or woman entire mental and moral physical activity. In other words, the heart is used for the hidden springs of the personal life. The Bible describes, the corrupt act as in the "heart",

because sin is a principle which has its seat in the centre of man/woman inward life, and then it will " defiles" as stated in Matthew 15:19a " for out of the heart proceed evil thoughts", which is the whole circuit of his action, evil thoughts proceed out of the heart. I Peter 3:4 a "BUT LET IT BE THE HIDDEN MAN OF THE HEART". It represents the true character but conceals it. According to St John 14:1" LET NOT YOUR HEART BE TROUBLED: YE BELIEVE IN GOD, BELIEVE ALSO IN ME" denotes the seat of physical life, James 5:5 a "YE HAVE LIVED IN PLEASURE ON THE EARTH, AND BEEN WANTON", denotes living in pleasure on the earth. The seat of moral nature and spiritual life and the seat of grief.

2. **YOU MUST ENCOURAGE YOURSELF** I Samuel 30:6 " and David was to distressed for the people spoke of stoning him, because of the soul of all the people was grieved, everyman for his sons and daughters; but David encouraged himself in the Lord his God". Just as David encouraged himself; he was urged to move forward, he was persuaded indicating a particular interest of encouragement. Encouragement is also to comfort, consolation, exhortation and entreaty. When David was distressed; he had inward pressure, anguish and had some affliction. David at that time had at least 600 men that just arrived at Ziklag from Aphek,

they were about three days away, and when they arrived they found out their hometown was burned, their wives and children were taken captive. The men were heart-broken because they felt some of the men should have stayed back to save their families. This is when David's follower spoke of stoning him. Try to imagine how David's grief, regret and exhaustion must have been. So David in spite of all his experience found strength in the Lord, "David Encouraged himself in the Lord his God".

3. **I WILL SHEW YOU A MYSTERY** I Corinthians 15:51" Behold I will shew you a mystery; We shall not all sleep, but we shall all be changed. Mystery in the English Dictionary means, a religious truth that one can know only by revelation and cannot fully be understood. And in the Vine's Expository Dictionary, it states that which being outside the range of assisted natural comprehension, can be made known by Divine Revelation, and is made known in a manner and at a time appointed by God. In the ordinary sense mystery can imply knowledge that is withheld, and associated with" made known"; that which is" manifested", that which is "revealed", and" understood". So when Jesus said, I'll shew you a mystery, he is revealing that which should be made known or understand his divine knowledge. I Corinthian 13:2" AND

THOUGH I HAVE THE GIFT OF PROPHECY AND UNDERSTAND ALL MYSTERIES AND ALL KNOWLEDGE; AND THOUGH I HAVE ALL FAITH, SO THAT I COULD REMOVE MOUNTAINS, AND HAVE NOT CHARITY, I AM NOTHING" I Corinthians 2:7a" BUT WE SPEAK THE WISDOM OF GOD IN A MYSTERY", even the hidden wisdom. Ephesians 1:9a "HAVING MADE KNOWN TO US THE MYSTERY OF HIS WILL. Ephesians 3:3a" HOW THAT BY REVELATION HE MADE KNOWN TO ME THE MYSTERY"

4. **When ye drink any deadly thing:** St Mark 16:18a "they shall take up serpents, and if they drink any deadly thing; is ministering to those who belong to Christ and by doing so virtually toward Him. According to James 3:8," but the tongue can no man tame; it is an unruly evil, full of deadly poison" according to researcher, all species have been tamed by man, but the tongue no man can tame except by the Holy Spirit dwells inside. St Luke 10:19 "Behold, I give unto you power to tread on serpents and scorpions, and over all the power of the enemy: and nothing shall by any means hurt you". To tread upon means to have absolute mastery over. Christians are to have power (authority) over all the power of the devil and nothing shall hurt you. We must understand that this does not imply freedom from physical or

material injury. "Serpents and Scorpions" all power of the enemy refers to demons power primarily. The whole passage is speaking of "Devils, Satan, Serpents, Scorpions, Power of the Enemy Spirits. This is where power over demons should not be your source of joy, but merely sonship evidence by one's name being written in the Lambs Book of Life.

5. **Faith as the grain of a mustard seed:** Matthews 17:20b "And Jesus said unto them, Because of your unbelief: for verily, I say unto you, If ye have faith as a grain of mustard seed, ye shall say unto this mountain, Remove hence to yonder place; Jesus is saying nothing shall be impossible, the will of God governs all things, this is the promise. The mustard seed being the least of all seeds, but when it is grown, it is the greatest of all herbs. The mustard seed have conditions to be fulfilled, a small seed sown in the earth, grows larger than garden herbs, having large branches and becomes a tree. The mustard are annuals, reproduced with an extraordinary, rapidity, it is the greatest among all herbs in the forest. It is like a grain of mustard seed, which when is sown in the earth is less than all seed in the earth, this parable illustrates the abnormal growth of the Kingdom of God among men. Instead of remaining a refuge for true believers, it was to become a

place for ungodly men and professed Christians. Then St Luke 13:19 "It is like a grain of mustard, which a man took, and cast into his garden; and it grew, and waxed a great tree; and the fowls of the air lodged in the branches there of". This is where the mustard seed in Palestinian grows in one season to a shrub the size of a tree.

6. **Faith without works is dead:** James 2:26 "for as the body without the spirit is dead, so faith without works is dead also" faith is a conviction made upon hearing—to persuade through spiritual belief. Therefore, the main elements in faith are in relations to the visible God, as distinct from faith in man. There are several statements that correspond to faith. 1. A firm conviction which produces an acknowledgement of Gods' revelation or his truth. II Thessalonians 2:12 "that they might all be damned who believed not the truth; but had pleasure in unrighteousness". 2. A personal surrender to Him; John 1:12 "But as many as received him, to them gave the power to become the sons of god, even to them that believe on his name". The object of Abraham's faith was not God's promise, but that his faith rested on God Himself." The body will only die at the sign of physical death, done only when the soul and spirit leaves the body. The body then is returns to the dust of the earth and the soul and

spirit of the righteous goes to a resting place. Philippians 1:21, "for to me to live be Christ and to die is gain.

The inner man leaves the body at physical death and is no longer with the body, therefore, faith without works is dead (separated) and become powerless.

7. **Pray and Believe** St Mark 11:24 "Therefore, I say unto you, what things soever ye desire, when ye pray, believe that ye receive them, and ye shall have them." Several conditions of your prayers being answered 1. Refuse to doubt in your heart 2. Believe that whatsoever is asked is already granted. 3. Never say, "If it be they will concern anything you ask that is already the promise of God in His word. Have a clean heart and life with God and man.

Faith is essential to prayer; Matthew 21:22" and all things, whatsoever ye shall ask in prayer, believing ye shall receive." For faith are the recognition and our faithfulness to God. Matthew 7:7" ask, and it shall be given you; seek, and ye shall find; knock, and it shall be opened unto you."

MAY THE WILL OF GOD RICHLY BLESS AND KEEP

YOU AND MAY YOUR FAITH INCREASE DAY BY DAY AND YOU READ WITH AN UNDERSTANDING OF WHAT GOD IS SAYING UNTO THEE, AS YOU WALK THORUGH HIS WORD. AMEN

www.ingramcontent.com/pod-product-compliance
Lightning Source LLC
Chambersburg PA
CBHW060935050426
42453CB00009B/1021